HORSES

BY BLANCHE CHENERY PERRIN

Pictures by Hamilton Greene

GOLDEN PRESS
Western Publishing Company, Inc.
Racine, Wisconsin

Fourth Printing, 1972

© Copyright 1962 by Western Publishing Company, Inc.
All rights reserved. Produced in U.S.A.

GOLDEN, A LITTLE GOLDEN BOOK®, and GOLDEN PRESS®
are trademarks of Western Publishing Company, Inc.

A foal is a baby horse. Boy foals are called colts; girls are fillies.

Foals are not like human babies who mostly sleep and eat. A foal can stand up on its wobbly legs and walk beside its mother a few hours after it is born.

Foals love to play a game that looks like tag. They run up and down fields and kick up their heels. But if anything frightens a foal, it runs quickly to its mother and hides behind her.

When foals are naughty the mother nips them to make them behave themselves.

Horses come in different sizes. Some are very big, taller than a tall man.

Race horses and riding horses are medium size. Smallest of all are the ponies.

The gentle Shetland pony is the tiniest of all. Sometimes he is not much bigger than a large dog.

The Shetland pony is called the "children's friend" because children love to ride him. He is clever and friendly, and playful, too.

His coat is thick and he has a long, shaggy mane and tail to keep him snug in winter.

The speediest horses come from Arabia. Arabians called them "Drinkers of the Wind" because they ran so fast. They are reddish-brown, gray or black, with long, silky manes and flashing eyes.

Horse-racing used to be called the sport of kings. In the seventeenth century King James of England started the first racing stables. Horse-racing was so expensive that only kings and queens could afford it.

Here is Man O' War, the most famous American race horse. He won almost every race he entered.

Race horses run very swiftly. A racer can run three miles in the time it takes a man to run one mile.

Horses that are used for hunting are called hunters. A hunter is fearless. He loves the sound of the horn. He follows the fox over fields and hills and leaps high fences and wide ditches.

Justin Morgan was a famous American saddle horse, named after his owner. He was small but very strong and intelligent. He could easily carry a heavy man or pull large logs.

Perhaps you know the song about him. It begins "Justin Morgan had a horse . . ."

The Tennessee walking horse is another saddle horse, famous for his rocking-chair gait. He can carry his master comfortably all day.

A mounted policeman needs a good, steady saddle horse. So does the Queen when she reviews her troops. The horses they ride are especially trained to keep calm in noisy, swirling traffic.

A Shire horse is descended from the great war horses. Proud knights in heavy armor charged into battle riding these brave horses.

The Shire horse grows long hair on his lower legs. This is called "feather." He is tall and very strong. Shire horses are still used on some farms today.

Polo is a ball game played on horseback.

A good polo pony can start off at a gallop, stop and swivel around in his own length. A polo pony loves this exciting game and has lots of courage.

Snowball is a circus horse. His trainer chose him because he is clever and easily learns difficult tricks. Snowball can stand on his hind legs and nod his head gaily in time to music.

Postmen bring the mail today. A hundred years ago, mail was carried by the Pony Express, which started in Missouri. The ponies had to cross mountains and deserts. It took them eight days to reach California.

The beautiful Palomino is "the golden horse of the West." His coat is gold or cream and he has a light mane and tail.

The Palomino knows that he is beautiful and likes to show off.

Pinto means painted horse. Pintos are gaily splotched black or brown and white. Indians like to ride these tough horses.

They also like the Appaloosa horse, which has a white coat with brown or black spots.

Spaniards brought the first horses to our country. Some horses ran away from their masters. They found plenty of food and their numbers grew like Jack's beanstalk.

Indians caught some of these wild horses or mustangs and learned to ride. Indians made wonderful horsemen. They rode bareback and raced like the wind.

Bronco means rough and rude. The wildest mustangs are called broncos. A bronco hates to be ridden. He bucks and twists and jumps, trying to throw his rider off.

Some broncos are trained by cowboys, who use them to round up herds of cattle.

Some horses are still wild. They live in many parts of the world. There are still a few wild horses in our West.

Wild horses love their freedom and roam the land in large herds.

Zebras are cousins of horses. You can see them in a zoo. They have gay black and white stripes. Zebras are very difficult to tame.

The donkey or burro is also a cousin of the horse. The mule is half horse, half donkey. The donkey and mule make very good workers because they are strong and can work in the hot sun. Their song is a frequent and noisy bray.

These are the clothes that horses wear.

A Bridle. The bit goes in the horse's mouth. The rider gently holds the reins to guide him.

The Saddle. This makes a comfortable seat for the rider. He puts his feet in the stirrups. A blanket goes under the saddle to keep it from rubbing the horse's back.

Shoes. Horses wear shoes. A race horse's shoes are made of aluminum because it is light. Other horses wear iron. Shoes are nailed on. This does not hurt the horse's hooves—it protects them.

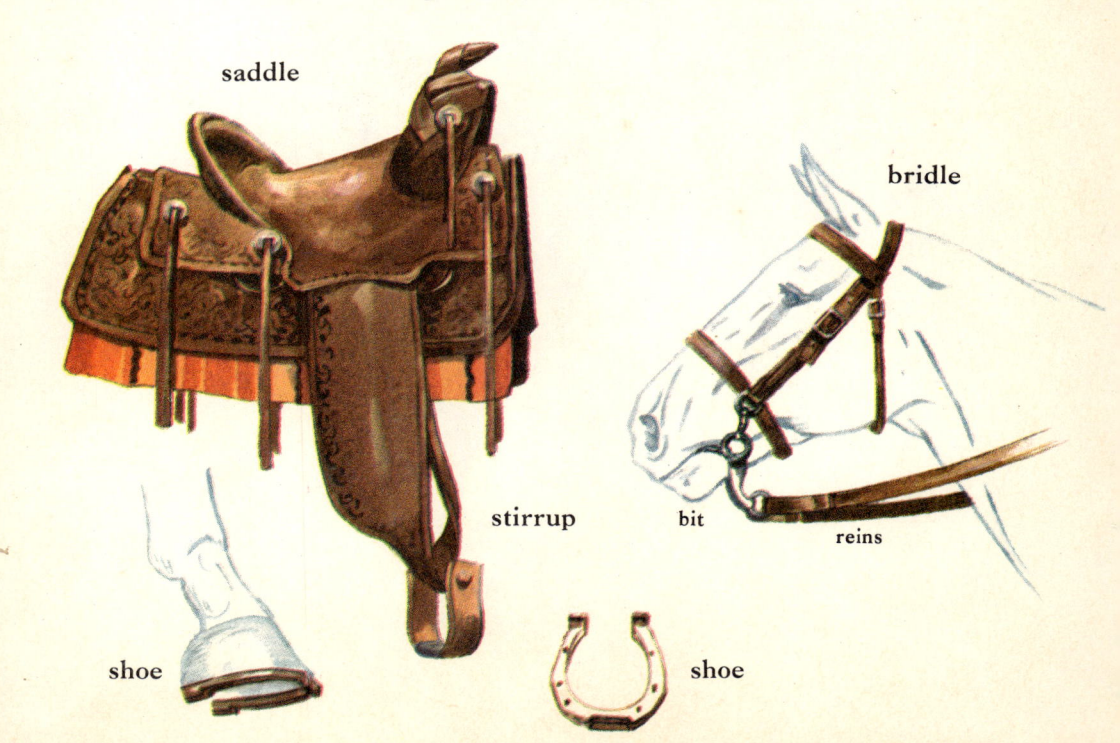